Riding a motorcycle is like turning the pages of a thrilling novel; each twist of the throttle propels you into a new chapter of adventure. In the world of motorcycles and reading, the engine roars with the echoes of stories written on the open road. Every ride is a journey, and every book is a roadmap to exploration. Embrace the wind, ignite your passion, and let the pages of both books and bikes transport you to realms where the spirit of freedom and discovery intertwine.

Sarita Hafit

OUR TRIVIA BOOKS

CONTENT

INTRODUCTION 4
THE HISTORY OF MOTORCYCLE 5
   ANSWERS 9
THE WORLD OF MOTOCROSS 10
   ANSWERS 12
AMERICAN MOTORCYCLES 13
   ANSWERS 16
MOTOCROSS RULES AND EQUIPEMENT 17
   ANSWERS 20
WORLD CHAMPIONSHIP 1996 21
   ANSWERS 25
1997 WORLD MOTORCYCLE CHAMPIONSHIP 25
   ANSWERS 29
WORLD SUPERBIKES 29
   ANSWERS 32
WORLD SUPERBIKE CHAMPIONSHIP TRIVIA 32
   ANSWERS 37
THE 2003 GRAND PRIX RIDERS TRIVIA 38
   ANSWERS 41
THE LIFE OF VALENTINO ROSSI 41
   ANSWERS 44
MOTORCYCLE ROADRACING RIDERS AND BIKES 44
   ANSWERS 48
UK SPEEDWAY FOR BEGINNERS 49
   ANSWERS 52
MOTORCYCLE ROADRACING NICKNAMES 53
   ANSWERS 55
SPEEDWAY: IDENTIFYING LEAGUE TEAM NICKNAMES 56
   ANSWERS 59
TT RACES ON THE ISLE OF MAN 60
   ANSWERS 62
ISLE BE BACK 63
   ANSWERS 66
VALENTINO ROSSI: FORZA DOTTORE TRIVIA 66
   ANSWERS 69
A LONG TIME AGO: GIACOMO AGOSTINI TRIVIA! 70
   ANSWERS 72
TRAVIS PASTRANA TRIVIA 73
   ANSWERS 75
SPEEDWAY - FROM THE BEGINNING! 75
   ANSWERS 78
SPEEDWAY TEAM'S NICKNAMES 78

ANSWERS	81
SUPERCROSS TRIVIA	**81**
ANSWERS	83
ATV TRIVIA	**84**
ANSWERS	86
MOTORCYCLE ROAD RACING TRIVIA	**86**
ANSWERS	88
SWINDON SPEEDWAY 2008	**89**
ANSWERS	91
BRITISH SPEEDWAY 2009	**91**
ANSWERS	93
ROAD BIKE RACING IN 2003	**94**
ANSWERS	96
FREESTYLE MOTOCROSS	**96**
ANSWERS	100
THE BERWICK BANDITS	**101**
ANSWERS	102
MOTORCYCLE IN CINEMA	**102**
ANSWERS	106

Introduction

Motorcycle Trivia Book is a thrilling journey through the heart-pounding world of motorcycles, meticulously curated with 360 Multiple Choice Questions that delve into the rich tapestry of motorcycling history, culture, and sport. Whether you're a seasoned biker, a motocross enthusiast, or simply captivated by the roar of engines, this book promises an exhilarating ride.

Embark on an exploration of The History of Motorcycles, tracing the evolution of these powerful machines from their inception to the present day. Navigate the challenging terrain of Motocross, learn about American motorcycles that have left an indelible mark, and unravel the excitement of World Superbikes. Immerse yourself in the thrills of motorcycle championships, from the historic 1996 World Championship to the intense battles of 2003 Grand Prix Riders.

Discover the ins and outs of Speedway racing, unravel the mysteries of TT Races on the Isle of Man, and delve into the iconic moments of motorcycle road racing. Get up close and personal with legendary riders like Valentino Rossi and Giacomo Agostini, and test your knowledge on motocross daredevil Travis Pastrana.

From the adrenaline-pumping Supercross to the daring feats of Freestyle Motocross, this book covers it all. Join us as we explore the intersection of motorcycles and cinema, unravel the stories behind Speedway Team's Nicknames, and reminisce about the unforgettable moments in the Swindon Speedway 2008 and British Speedway 2009.

This Ultimate Motorcycles Facts Book is not just a trivia book; it's a celebration of the passion, history, and culture that make motorcycles an enduring symbol of freedom and adventure. So, rev up your engines and prepare for a riveting ride through the fascinating world of motorcycles!

The History of Motorcycle

1. Who is often credited with building the first true motorcycle?
   a. Harley Davidson
   b. Gottlieb Daimler
   c. Kawasaki
   d. Ducati

2. In what year did the first commercially successful motorcycle, the Hildebrand & Wolfmüller, become available?
   a. 1885
   b. 1894
   c. 1903
   d. 1910

3. Which motorcycle company is known for introducing the first mass-produced motorcycle with a V-twin engine?
   a. Indian Motorcycle
   b. Triumph
   c. Honda
   d. BMW Motorrad

4. What was the first motorcycle to feature an electric starter, eliminating the need for a kickstarter?
   a. Harley-Davidson Sportster
   b. Yamaha YZF-R1
   c. Honda Goldwing
   d. Kawasaki Ninja

5. Which motorcycle company is credited with popularizing the concept of the "chopper" style in the 1960s?
   a. Ducati
   b. Honda
   c. Harley-Davidson
   d. Suzuki

6. What year did the iconic Harley-Davidson Fat Boy motorcycle make its debut?
   a. 1980
   b. 1990
   c. 2000
   d. 2010

7. Which motorcycle manufacturer introduced the first anti-lock braking system (ABS) on a production motorcycle?
   a. BMW Motorrad
   b. Honda
   c. Yamaha
   d. Kawasaki

8. In what decade did the concept of the superbike emerge, featuring high-performance motorcycles for the road?
   a. 1950s
   b. 1960s
   c. 1970s
   d. 1980s

9. Who is often credited with developing the first motorcycle helmet in the early 20th century?
a. T.E. Lawrence
b. Evel Knievel
c. Gottlieb Daimler
d. Lawrence of Arabia

10. Which motorcycle company introduced the first mass-produced motorcycle with fuel injection?
a. Suzuki
b. Yamaha
c. Honda
d. Kawasaki

11. What iconic motorcycle event began in 1907 and is often considered the oldest off-road motorcycle race in the world?
a. Isle of Man TT
b. Dakar Rally
c. Motocross of Nations
d. Erzberg Rodeo

12. In what year did Yamaha introduce the Yamaha VMAX, a muscle cruiser known for its powerful V4 engine?
a. 1985
b. 1995
c. 2005
d. 2015

13. Which motorcycle company is credited with popularizing the use of aluminum twin-spar frames in sportbikes?
a. Ducati
b. Kawasaki
c. Suzuki
d. Yamaha

14. What was the first motorcycle brand to implement electronic fuel injection on its sportbike models?
a. Honda
b. Yamaha
c. Kawasaki
d. Suzuki

15. In what year did the first three-wheeled motorcycle, known as a trike, become commercially available?
a. 1910
b. 1930
c. 1950
d. 1970

Answers

1. Gottlieb Daimler
2. 1903
3. Indian Motorcycle
4. Honda Goldwing
5. Harley-Davidson
6. 1990
7. BMW Motorrad
8. 1970s
9. T.E. Lawrence
10. Suzuki
11. Isle of Man TT
12. 1995
13. Suzuki
14. Suzuki
15. 1910

The World of Motocross

1. What is the term for the mogul-like section on a motocross track, which comprises 10 or more consecutive small jumps?
   a. In field
   b. Washboard
   c. Whoops
   d. Rhythm

2. What is the term for the dirt or debris thrown into the air by the spinning rear tire during riding?
   a. Flak
   b. Pitch
   c. Roost
   d. Spray

3. What is a common cause of "Arm Pump" experienced during riding?
   a. Riders gripping the handle bars too tightly
   b. Incorrect landing off a double jump
   c. Lack of calcium in the diet
   d. Riding too soon after eating

4. In motocross races, when riders line up at the starting gate and all gates drop simultaneously, the racer who earns the "hole shot" is the first to accomplish what?
   a. Complete the first lap
   b. Completely clear the starting gate

c. Reach the first corner
   d. Clear the first double jump

5. Motocross racers often sport vibrant colors and designs. What brand of motorcycle is recognized for its distinctive bright green color?
   a. Suzuki
   b. KTM
   c. Honda
   d. Kawasaki

6. Who is the former national rider, once hailed as the King of Supercross, and credited with innovating the trick known as the "nac-nac"?
   a. Jeremy McGrath
   b. Ricky Charmichael
   c. Travis Pastrana
   d. Brian Deegan

7. What early national motocross rider was commonly known by the nickname "Hurricane"?
   a. Gary Semics
   b. Jeff Ward
   c. Bob Hannah
   d. Marty Smith

8. Among the listed riders, who was the first to secure a National Championship?
   a. Jeremy McGrath
   b. Chad Reed
   c. Jeff Ward
   d. Mike LaRocco

9. Which outdoor motocross class was discontinued in the 1990s?
a. 500cc
b. 125cc
c. 250cc
d. MX lite

10. What is the endearing term for the tire pattern on motocross bikes?
a. Knobbies
b. Treaddies
c. Race slicks
d. Muddies

Answers

1. Whoops
2. Roost
3. Riders gripping the handle bars too tightly
4. Reach the first corner
5. Kawasaki
6. Jeremy McGrath
7. Bob Hannah
8. Jeff Ward
9. 500cc
10. Knobbies

American motorcycles

1. Who co-founded Harley-Davidson, one of the most iconic American motorcycle manufacturers?
   a. William S. Harley
   b. Arthur Davidson
   c. Walter Davidson
   d. All of the above

2. In what year was the Harley-Davidson Motor Company officially established?
   a. 1901
   b. 1903
   c. 1910
   d. 1920

3. What was the nickname given to the Harley-Davidson motorcycles used by the U.S. military during World War II?
   a. Iron Horse
   b. War Eagle
   c. Wartime Hog
   d. Jeep Bike

4. Which American motorcycle company introduced the iconic Indian Chief motorcycle in the 1920s?
   a. Harley-Davidson
   b. Indian Motorcycle Company

c. Excelsior-Henderson
d. Crocker Motorcycle Company

5. What was the first model produced by the company that eventually became the Indian Motorcycle Company?
a. Indian Chief
b. Indian Scout
c. Indian Four
d. Indian Powerplus

6. What American motorcycle brand is known for its production of heavyweight cruisers like the Road King and Fat Boy?
a. Indian Motorcycle
b. Harley-Davidson
c. Victory Motorcycles
d. Excelsior-Henderson

7. Which American motorcycle manufacturer produced the "Captain America" bike featured in the movie "Easy Rider" (1969)?
a. Harley-Davidson
b. Indian Motorcycle Company
c. Triumph
d. Norton

8. In what year did the iconic Harley-Davidson Sportster model make its debut?
a. 1957
b. 1969
c. 1972

d. 1980

9. What motorcycle brand did Evel Knievel famously ride during his career as a daredevil stunt performer?
a. Harley-Davidson
b. Indian Motorcycle Company
c. Triumph
d. Kawasaki

10. Which American motorcycle company introduced the first mass-produced V-twin engine motorcycle?
a. Harley-Davidson
b. Indian Motorcycle Company
c. Excelsior-Henderson
d. Cleveland Motorcycle Manufacturing Company

11. What was the name of the first American motorcycle race held in 1903, which was won by Harley-Davidson?
a. Daytona 200
b. Springfield Mile
c. Motogiro America
d. Hendee Manufacturing Trophy Race

12. Which American motorcycle manufacturer produced the X-75 Hurricane, a distinctive triple-engine bike designed by Craig Vetter?
a. Harley-Davidson
b. Indian Motorcycle Company
c. Triumph
d. BSA

13. What was the name of the motorcycle brand founded by George M. Hendee in 1901, which later merged with Indian Motorcycle Company?
a. Excelsior Motor Manufacturing & Supply Company
b. Henderson Motorcycle Company
c. Cyclone Motorcycle Company
d. Thor Motorcycle Company

14. In what year did the iconic Harley-Davidson Electra Glide make its debut, featuring a distinctive "batwing" fairing?
a. 1957
b. 1965
c. 1970
d. 1980

15. Which American motorcycle manufacturer is known for producing the first American-built sportbike, the Buell Lightning?
a. Harley-Davidson
b. Indian Motorcycle Company
c. Excelsior-Henderson
d. Buell Motorcycle Company

Answers

1. All of the above
2. 1903
3. Iron Horse

4. Indian Motorcycle Company
5. Indian Powerplus
6. Harley-Davidson
7. Harley-Davidson
8. 1957
9. Harley-Davidson
10. Excelsior-Henderson
11. Hendee Manufacturing Trophy Race
12. Harley-Davidson
13. Excelsior Motor Manufacturing & Supply Company
14. 1970
15. Buell Motorcycle Company

Motocross Rules And Equipement

1. What is the maximum allowable engine size for a 250cc class motocross bike?
a. 250cc
b. 300cc
c. 450cc
d. 500cc

2. In motocross racing, what is the purpose of a holeshot device?
a. Enhance suspension performance
b. Improve fuel efficiency
c. Assist with quick starts

d. Increase top speed

3. **Which safety gear is mandatory for all motocross riders during a race?**
   a. Elbow pads
   b. Knee pads
   c. Chest protector
   d. Neck brace

4. **What is the maximum allowable number of riders on the track during a motocross race?**
   a. 15
   b. 20
   c. 25
   d. 30

5. **What type of tires are commonly used in motocross racing for better traction on various terrains?**
   a. Slick tires
   b. Street tires
   c. Knobby tires
   d. All-weather tires

6. **How many laps are typically in a standard motocross race?**
   a. 5
   b. 10
   c. 15
   d. 20

7. **In motocross, what is the purpose of the red flag?**
   a. Start the race

b. Signal the end of the race
c. Stop the race due to a serious incident
d. Indicate a rider's position on the track

8. Which organization is responsible for setting the rules and regulations for professional motocross racing?
a. FIM (Fédération Internationale de Motocyclisme)
b. AMA (American Motorcyclist Association)
c. MXGP (Motocross Grand Prix)
d. X Games

9. What is the minimum age requirement for participating in professional motocross events?
a. 16
b. 18
c. 21
d. 25

10.   Which of the following is NOT a standard motocross track feature?
a. Whoops
b. Tabletops
c. Hairpin turns
d. Banked corners

11.   What is the purpose of a tear-off in motocross goggles?
a. Improve aerodynamics
b. Enhance visibility
c. Reduce glare
d. Protect against dust and debris

12. What is the maximum allowable decibel level for motocross bikes during a race?
a. 90 dB
b. 100 dB
c. 110 dB
d. 120 dB

13. Which of the following is a violation that could lead to disqualification in motocross racing?
a. Excessive tire wear
b. Jumping the start
c. Low fuel level
d. Helmet visor obstruction

14. What is the purpose of the blue flag in motocross racing?
a. Indicate the leader of the race
b. Warn a rider they are about to be lapped
c. Signal the end of the race
d. Notify a rider of a mechanical issue

15. In motocross, what does the term "scrub" refer to?
a. Cleaning the bike
b. Clearing a jump with minimal air time
c. Applying a special type of lubricant
d. Adjusting the suspension

Answers

1. 250cc

2. Assist with quick starts
3. Chest protector
4. 20
5. Knobby tires
6. 15
7. Stop the race due to a serious incident
8. FIM (Fédération Internationale de Motocyclisme)
9. 18
10. Hairpin turns
11. Enhance visibility
12. 110 dB
13. Jumping the start
14. Warn a rider they are about to be lapped
15. Clearing a jump with minimal air time

World Championship 1996

1. In the 1996 World Championship, who claimed the title of 500cc World Champion?
   a. Mick Doohan
   b. Greg Hancock
   c. Hans Nielsen
   d. Jason Crump

2. In the 1996 World Championship, which motorcycle brand did Mick Doohan, team-mate Alex Criville, and Luca Cadalora all ride?

a. Kawasaki
b. Honda
c. Yamaha
d. Suzuki

3. Who emerged victorious in the inaugural round of the championship held at Shah Alam in Malaysia?
a. Mick Doohan
b. Tadayuki Okada
c. Alex Criville
d. Luca Cadalora

4. After the second race in Indonesia, who was at the forefront of the 500cc World Championship standings?
a. Max Biaggi
b. Mick Doohan
c. Alex Barros
d. Luca Cadalora

5. In the year 1996, how many podium finishes did Mick Doohan achieve?
a. 10
b. 14
c. 15
d. 12

6. Who secured their inaugural career victory in the 250cc class at the Brazilian Grand Prix?
a. Jean-Paul Ruggia
b. Tohru Ukawa
c. Olivier Jacque

d. Jurgen Fuchs

7. At the Czech Grand Prix, which eventual 125cc champion earned their first career victory?
a. Roberto Locatelli
b. Valentino Rossi
c. Emilio Alzamora
d. Ivan Goi

8. Who, after recovering from a severe injury, achieved a triumphant return with a third-place finish at the French 500cc Grand Prix at Paul Ricard?
a. Carlos Checa
b. Alberto Puig
c. Darryl Beattie
d. Scott Russell

9. At the conclusion of the season, what was the total point tally for Doohan?
a. 300
b. 309
c. 320
d. 327

10. How many instances did Mick Doohan and Alex Criville secure a 1-2 finish, regardless of their order, during the season?
a. 10
b. 7
c. 8
d. 6

11. In 1996, where was the Australian Grand Prix held?
a. Phillip Island
b. Eastern Creek
c. Sandown
d. Adelaide Street Circuit

12. How many instances did Honda motorcycles achieve a complete podium sweep with a 1-2-3 finish?
a. 6
b. 10
c. 8
d. 12

13. In 1996, who claimed the title of 250cc World Champion?
a. Tetsuya Harada
b. Ralf Waldmann
c. Max Biaggi
d. Olivier Jacque

14. Who won the 1996 125cc World Championship?
a. Stefano Perugini
b. Haruchika Aoki
c. Kazuto Sakata
d. Tomomi Manako

15. Spoiler Alert: Who emerged as the 1996 World Superbike Champion?
a. Troy Corser
b. Aaron Slight
c. Carl Fogarty

d. John Kocinski

Answers

1. Mick Doohan
2. Honda
3. Luca Cadalora
4. Alex Barros
5. 12
6. Olivier Jacque
7. Valentino Rossi
8. Alberto Puig
9. 309
10. 8
11. Eastern Creek
12. 8
13. Max Biaggi
14. Haruchika Aoki
15. Troy Corser

1997 World Motorcycle Championship

1. Which rider claimed the 1997 500cc World Championship title?
   a. Mick Doohan
   b. Wayne Rainey
   c. Alex Crivillé
   d. Kevin Schwantz

2. Who secured the 1997 250cc World Championship title?
   a. Olivier Jacque
   b. Tetsuya Harada
   c. Ralf Waldmann
   d. Max Biaggi

3. Who secured the 125cc World Championship title in 1997?
   a. Valentino Rossi
   b. Tomomi Manako
   c. Kazuto Sakata
   d. Haruchika Aoki

4. How many victories did Honda achieve in the 500cc class during the 1997 racing season?
   a. 12 of 15
   b. 14 of 15
   c. 15 of 15
   d. 13 of 15

5. Who emerged as the winner of the 250cc race in Japan in the year 1997?
   a. Daijiro Katoh
   b. Tohru Ukawa
   c. Tetsuya Harada
   d. Shinya Nakano

6. True or False: no other rider than Rossi and Ueda won a 125cc race in 1997?
   a. True
   b. False

7. Which groundbreaking motorcycle was introduced to the 500cc class in the year 1997?
   a. Muz
   b. Honda V-Twin
   c. Modenas KR3
   d. Elf 500

8. In which race did Taki Aoki achieve his highest result, securing second place during the 1997 500cc season?
   a. Australia
   b. Germany
   c. Imola
   d. Japan

9. In the 125cc class of 1997, which manufacturer did 'Nobby' Ueda ride for?
   a. Honda
   b. Yamaha
   c. Aprilia
   d. Italjet

10. Which 250cc rider managed to secure points in all 15 rounds during the 1997 season?
    a. Max Biaggi
    b. Ralf Waldmann
    c. Franco Battaini
    d. Tohru Ukawa

11. How many riders did the Lucky Strike Suzuki 500cc team employ during the 1997 season?

a. 5
b. 2
c. 4
d. 3

12. How many times did Mick Doohan secure pole position in the year 1997?
a. 13
b. 10
c. 12
d. 15

13. The 1997 125cc Manufacturers Championship was the _____ that Aprilia claimed victory in?
a. 5th
b. 3rd
c. 2nd
d. 4th

14. During the 1997 season, how many consecutive races did Doohan emerge victorious in?
a. 10
b. 8
c. 12
d. 6

15. Without giving away any spoilers, who emerged as the World Superbike champion in 1997?
a. Troy Corser
b. Carl Fogarty
c. John Kocinski
d. Scott Russell

Answers

1. Michael Doohan
2. Max Biaggi
3. Valentino Rossi
4. 15 of 15
5. Daijiro Katoh
6. True
7. Modenas KR3
8. Australia
9. Honda
10. Ralf Waldmann
11. 4
12. 13
13. 2nd
14. 10
15. John Kocinski

World Superbikes

1. In 1990, who secured victory in the World Superbike Championship?
   a. Fabrizio Pirovano
   b. Raymond Roche
   c. Stephane Mertens
   d. Rob Phillis

2. How many times did Carl Fogarty clinch the World championship title in the 20th century?
a. 5
b. 4
c. 3
d. 2

3. In which English county was Carl Fogarty born?
a. Lancashire
b. Cumbria
c. Yorkshire
d. Northumberland

4. In the year 2002, who held the title of World Champion?
a. Ben Bostrum
b. Troy Bayliss
c. Colin Edwards
d. Noriyuki Haga

5. By the conclusion of the 2002 season, how many individuals had earned the title of World Superbike Champion?
a. 8
b. 9
c. 7
d. 6

6. By the conclusion of the 2002 season, how many Australians had secured victory in the World Superbike Championship?

a. 1
b. 3
c. 2
d. 4

7. What is the name of the Superbike team founded by Carl Fogarty, set to make its debut in the 2003 racing season?
a. Foggy-Ducati Racing
b. Foggy-Petronas Racing
c. Foggy No.1 Racing
d. King Carl Racing

8. Up until the 2002 season's conclusion, which manufacturer had secured the World Superbike Championship title the most times among the following options?
a. Yamaha
b. Honda
c. Ducati
d. Kawazaki

9. At which racing circuit did Carl Fogarty sustain an injury that eventually led to his retirement from racing?
a. Laguna Seca, USA
b. Phillip Island, Australia
c. Kyalami, South Africa
d. Valencia, Spain

10. Which motorcycle did Colin Edwards ride to win the championship in the year 2000?

a. Ducati 966
b. Honda SP1
c. Ducati 916
d. Kawazaki ZX7RR

Answers

1. Raymond Roche
2. 4
3. Lancashire
4. Colin Edwards
5. 9
6. 2
7. Foggy-Petronas Racing
8. Ducati
9. Phillip Island, Australia
10. Honda SP1

World Superbike Championship Trivia

1. What is the 2002 world champion Colin Edwards also known as?
   a. Texas Tornado
   b. Speedy Edwards
   c. Moto Maestro
   d. Racing Raptor

2. Who emerged as Carl Fogarty's main competitor in the year 1994?
   a. John Kocinski

b. Pierfrancesco Chili
  c. Scott Russell
  d. Aaron Slight

3. **Which motorcycle, not from Honda or Ducati, secured a world championship victory prior to Edwards' Honda in 2002?**
  a. Suzuki
  b. Kawasaki
  c. Aprilia
  d. Yamaha

4. **In which year did the Aprilia RSV-R1000 make its first appearance?**
  a. 1997
  b. 1999
  c. 2000
  d. 2001

5. **Which track, featured in the World Superbike Championship in the 20th century, holds the record as the longest?**
  a. Laguna Seca
  b. Phillip Island
  c. Hockenheim
  d. Assen

6. **Before Carl Fogarty secured the title in 1994, who held the distinction of being the most successful British rider in World Superbikes?**
  a. Terry Rymer
  b. John Reynolds
  c. Steve Hislop
  d. James Whitham

7. At which racetrack did Carl Fogarty experience a crash in the first race, resulting in injuries to his hands and feet, yet he managed to come back and win the second race of the day?
a. Monza
b. Sugo
c. Kyalami
d. Albacete

8. On which renowned circuit can the 'corkscrew' be found?
a. Donington Park
b. Brands Hatch
c. Laguna Seca
d. Imola

9. Which Japanese Superbike standout experienced a major accident at the USA round of the championship in 1998, nearly compelling him to consider retirement?
a. Hitayatsu Izutzu
b. Noriyuki Haga
c. Akira Yanagawa
d. Akira Ryo

10. Until 1992, which accomplished team manager also rode for Bimota/Ducati?
a. Neil Tuxworth
b. Davide Tardozzi
c. Nigel Bosworth
d. Virginio Ferrari

11. Who emerged as the victor in the inaugural World Superbike Championship in 1988?

a. Doug Polen
b. Fred Merkel
c. Raymond Roche
d. Scott Russell

12. Which factory Ducati rider was associated with the number 155 until a challenging 2002 season?
a. Carl Fogarty
b. Rubén Xaus
c. Troy Corser
d. Ben Bostrom

13. Which pair of riders inked deals to compete for Foggy Petronas Racing in 2003?
a. Troy Corser & James Toseland
b. Troy Corser & James Haydon
c. James Toseland & Troy Bayliss
d. James Haydon & Chris Walker

14. True or False: When Neil Hodgson rode for the GSE ducati team, he never won a race outside of the UK.
a. True
b. False

15. At which circuit did Troy Bayliss have a crash, paving the way for Colin Edwards to contend for the 2002 title?
a. Assen
b. Brands Hatch
c. Imola
d. Oschersleben

16. Who, being a close rival of Carl Fogarty, threw a punch at him in the pits after alleging that Foggy had forced him onto the grass in 1997?

a. Mike Hale
b. Colin Edwards
c. Pierfrancesco Chili
d. John Kocinski

17. Who, before the conclusion of the 20th century, held the distinction of being the youngest rider to clinch a Superbike world title?
a. Troy Bayliss
b. Doug Polen
c. John Kocinski
d. Fred Merkel

18. Who is the Australian rider recognized as a 'wet weather specialist,' capable of outpacing championship leaders in damp conditions?
a. Anthony Gobert
b. Broc Parkes
c. Troy Bayliss
d. Peter Goddard

19. Who quickly gained a reputation as one of the most fearless and aggressive riders when he burst onto the scene in 1998?
a. Gregorio Lavilla
b. Simon Crafar
c. Ruben Xaus
d. Noriyuki Haga

20. Who secured the title of the 2002 British Superbike champion (not the world champion)?
a. Michael Rutter
b. Steve Hislop
c. Steve Plater
d. Sean Emmett

Answers

1. Texas Tornado
2. Scott Russell
3. Kawasaki
4. 1999
5. Hockenheim
6. Terry Rymer
7. Sugo
8. Laguna Seca
9. Akira Yanagawa
10. Davide Tardozzi
11. Fred Merkel
12. Ben Bostrom
13. Troy Corser & James Haydon
14. True
15. Assen
16. Pierfrancesco Chili
17. Troy Corser
18. Anthony Gobert
19. Noriyuki Haga
20. Steve Hislop

The 2003 Grand Prix Riders Trivia

1. Among the notable speedway riders of the 90s and 2000s, Tony Rickardsson stands out for winning five out of his first ten grand prixs. However, in the 1970s, a distinguished New Zealand rider claimed six world titles. Can you identify this rider?
   a. Bruce Penhall
   b. Ove Fundin
   c. Soren Sjosten
   d. Ivan Mauger

2. Mark Loram, Britain's standout rider of the 1990s and the 2000 world champion, was, surprisingly, born on a Mediterranean island. Which specific island was it?
   a. Malta
   b. Sardinia
   c. Cyprus
   d. Crete

3. While Jason Crump assumed the position of Australian number one in 2001, he was originally born in Bristol. Following in the footsteps of his renowned speedway father, can you recall his father's name, who also held the title of Australian number one?
   a. Mike Crump
   b. Ted Crump
   c. Jim Crump
   d. Phil Crump

4. Bo Brhel, the Czech rider, achieved the distinction of being the oldest participant in the 2003 speedway grand prix at 37 years old. What is the name "Bo" abbreviated from?
   a. Bojangles
   b. Bohumil
   c. Bodin
   d. Boris

5. Tomasz Gollob is widely regarded as one of the greatest speedway riders who never clinched the world title. However, he holds a record for winning a particular grand prix multiple times. Which grand prix is it?
   a. Swedish
   b. Polish
   c. British
   d. Australian

6. Swedish rider Michael Max participated in the grand prix series under a different name, Michael Karlsson. What reason did he provide for changing his name for the 2003 grand prix?
   a. Sponsor, Max Racing, paid him to change it for season
   b. Fell out with father and now rides under mother's name
   c. Too many Karlssons in speedway
   d. Thought people would remember him better

7. Lukas Dryml, along with his brother Ales, has participated in the grand prix. However, Lukas was the sole representative in the 2003 series. Their father, who also competed in the world finals, bears what name?

a. Lukas Dryml
b. Ales Dryml
c. Mika Dryml
d. Alf Dryml

8. Ryan Sullivan, the Australian who claimed victory in the Swedish grand prix in 2003, competed for Peterborough in Britain, Kapana in Sweden, and Czestochowa in Poland. However, where was he residing during the 2003 season?
a. Peterborough
b. Czestochowas
c. Kapana
d. Munich

9. Greg Hancock, the American who secured the world championship in 1997 and the US national championship in 1998 and 2002, participated in the 2003 series for a British club. Can you identify the British club he rode for?
a. Didn't ride in Britain
b. Belle Vue
c. Wolverhampton
d. Eastbourne

10. Hans Andersen, the young Danish rider who held the 25th rank in the world at the beginning of 2003, had a notable season. How many clubs did he ride for during the 2003 season?
a. 4
b. 2
c. 3
d. 1

Answers

1. Ivan Mauger
2. Malta
3. Phil Crump
4. Bohumil
5. Polish
6. Too many Karlssons in speedway
7. Ales Dryml
8. Peterborough
9. Didn't ride in Britain
10. 4

The Life of Valentino Rossi

1. What is the birthdate of Valentino Rossi?
a. February 19, 1981
b. February 7, 1982
c. February 1, 1977
d. February 16, 1979

2. During which year did he achieve his first victory in the 125cc world championship race?
a. 1998
b. 1995
c. 1996
d. 1997

3. In his debut year, Valentino Rossi secured his first 500cc World Championship title.
   a. True
   b. False

4. Which among these practices is a customary pre-ride ritual of Valentino Rossi?
   a. Adjusting the fit of his leathers by standing straight up on the foot-pegs, whilst riding down the pit-lane
   b. Stopping about 2 metres from his bike, bending over and reaching his boots
   c. All of these
   d. When arriving at his bike, crouching down and holding the right-side foot-peg with his head bowed

5. What historical legend served as the inspiration for Valentino Rossi's celebration during the 1997 British Grand Prix?
   a. Henry VIII
   b. Tutankhamun
   c. Julius Caesar
   d. Robin Hood

6. Throughout his entire career, who has been Valentino Rossi's most formidable rival?
   a. Loris Capirossi
   b. Max Biaggi
   c. Alex Barros
   d. Carlos Checa

7. When Valentino Rossi transitioned from Honda to Yamaha in 2004, which highly regarded chief racing engineer joined him in the move?
a. Joesph Barnes
b. Jack Ball
c. Joshua Brackley
d. Jeremy Burgess

8. Which pair of natural elements prominently feature in Valentino Rossi's livery and helmet designs?
a. Earth & Moon
b. Wind & The Sea
c. Water & Fire
d. Sun & Moon

9. Which of the following is a popular nickname for Valentino Rossi?
a. The Scientist
b. The Lawyer
c. The Doctor
d. The Mechanic

10. Despite losing the championship to Nicky Hayden in 2006, how many race victories did Valentino Rossi secure during that season?
a. 4
b. 6
c. 5
d. 3

Answers

1. February 16, 1979
2. 1996
3. False
4. All of these
5. Robin Hood
6. Max Biaggi
7. Jeremy Burgess
8. Sun & Moon
9. The Doctor
10. 5

Motorcycle Roadracing Riders and Bikes

1. What was the first name of the esteemed racer, Mr. Hailwood?
a. Michael
b. Stanley
c. Reggie
d. Wooster

2. In which race course, one of the few still run on public roads, did Mr. Hailwood achieve some of his most celebrated victories?
a. Sebring
b. Mosport

c. The Isle of Man
d. The Isle of Wight

3. Following an 11-year hiatus from motorcycle racing, Mr. Hailwood secured victory in the IOM Senior TT, prompting the manufacturer of his race bike to create a street model to commemorate the win. Which company produced this bike?
a. MV Agusta
b. Ducati
c. Tohatsu
d. Harley-Davidson

4. Which American became the second to clinch a world road racing title?
a. Harvey Mushman
b. Steve Baker
c. Kenny Roberts Sr.
d. Wes Cooley

5. How many times did Randy Mamola secure the second position in the world rankings during his impressive career, despite never winning a world championship?
a. Four
b. Seven
c. One
d. None

6. What is the name of the individual who emulated his father by winning the world Grand Prix title?
a. Bob Hailwood
b. Caveat Emptor

c. John Surtees
d. Kenny Roberts Jr.

7. True or False: Eddie Lawson and Wayne Rainey, both born in southern California, achieved success as dirt-track racers, competed in 250s and Superbikes for Kawasaki, and secured multiple 500cc Grand Prix titles.
a. True
b. False

8. True or False: Harley Davidson built a competitive MotoGP bike from 1989-1992.
a. True
b. False

9. Which individual, victorious in both the AMA and World Superbike championships, shares their name with an early 20th-century motorcycle brand?
a. Floyd Henderson
b. Fred Merkel
c. Jimmy Crocker
d. Billy Boardtrack

10. Which exceptional individual from Northern Ireland, acclaimed as the "King of the Roads," achieved remarkable success in the realm of racing as a publican?
a. Joey Dunlop
b. Holden McGroin
c. Alf Langdon
d. Carl Fogarty

11. Which Norton model derived its name from a renowned racing location?
a. Dominator
b. Manx
c. Nurburgring
d. Electra

12. During the decline of the English motorcycle industry around 1970, the Rising Sun of Japan emerged with exciting bikes. Which Yamaha model became the dominant force in road racing worldwide during the 1970s?
a. X-6 Hustler
b. XS650
c. Virago
d. TZ750

13. True or False: Kenny Roberts raced a 2-stroke powered bike on a dirt track.
a. True
b. False

14. Which among these accomplished Australian racers has yet to secure a world championship?
a. Troy Corser
b. Wayne Gardner
c. Mat Mladin
d. Troy Bayliss

15. What is the last name of the racing family where both Father Floyd and son Don achieved

victories in the Daytona 200, while brothers Bob and Dave also participated in races there?
a. Vesco
b. Smith
c. Munro
d. Emde

Answers

1. Stanley
2. The Isle of Man
3. Ducati
4. Kenny Roberts Sr.
5. Four
6. Kenny Roberts Jr.
7. true
8. False
9. Fred Merkel
10. Joey Dunlop
11. Manx
12. TZ750
13. true
14. Mat Mladin
15. Emde

UK Speedway For Beginners

1. Among the following four elements, what is the singular feature shared by a speedway bike and an ordinary road bike, considering the various differences between the two?
   a. Gears
   b. Rear suspension
   c. Brakes
   d. Clutch

2. True or False: A speedway bike accelerates as fast as a Formula 1 racing car?
   a. True
   b. False

3. What fuel type powers speedway bikes?
   a. Ethanol
   b. Diesel
   c. Petrol
   d. Methanol

4. Apart from the GM engine, what was the other widely used type of engine among speedway riders?
   a. Kawasaki
   b. Yamaha

c. Jawa
d. Honda

5. **What kind of surface is typically found on a speedway track?**
a. Grass
b. Shale
c. Concrete
d. Sand

6. **From which country did speedway originate?**
a. Australia
b. Norway
c. Britain
d. Poland

7. **Which country did the six-time world champion Ivan Mauger hail from?**
a. Denmark
b. New Zealand
c. Sweden
d. Czech Republic

8. **Among these peculiar-sounding names, which one did not belong to a legitimate rider over the years?**
a. Bernt Persson
b. None of these
c. Reidar Eide
d. Beike Rida

9. **Which speedway team was referred to as the Pirates, considering that all speedway teams typically**

have nicknames, such as Peterborough's 'Panthers' and Sheffield's 'Tigers'?
a. Arena Essex
b. Poole
c. Hull
d. Somerset

10. What British speedway team was alternatively recognized as the Witches?
a. Wolverhampton
b. Workington
c. Eastbourne
d. Ipswich

11. True or False: Speedway races take place in a clockwise direction around the track?
a. True
b. False

12. What is the material composition of the protective race suits commonly referred to as kevlars worn by many riders?
a. Leather
b. Kevlar
c. Rubber
d. Nylon

13. Among these countries, which one lacks a recognized league structure for speedway?
a. Greece
b. Sweden
c. Poland

d. Denmark

14. In a typical British speedway league meeting, where two teams of 7 riders compete over 15 heats, how many riders participate in each heat?
a. 8
b. 2
c. 4
d. 6

15. By what nickname were the speedway team from Newcastle known?
a. Magpies
b. Aces
c. Diamonds
d. Knights

Answers

1. Clutch
2. True
3. Methanol
4. Jawa
5. Shale
6. Australia
7. New Zealand
8. Beike Rida
9. Poole
10. Ipswich
11. False
12. Kevlar
13. Greece
14. 4

15.   Diamonds

Motorcycle Roadracing Nicknames

1. Identified by the number 46 and renowned as "The Doctor," this Italian multiple world champion is arguably the most famous rider in history. Who is he?
a. Valentino Rossi
b. Eddie Lawson
c. Mick Doohan
d. Kenny Roberts

2. Which two-time World Superbike champion is known by the nickname "Texas Tornado"?
a. Troy Bayliss
b. Miguel Duhamel
c. Troy Corser
d. Colin Edwards

3. Hailing from Modesto, California, this three-time 500cc Grand Prix world champion is famously referred to as "The King." Who is he?
a. John Kocinski
b. Kenny Roberts Sr.
c. Wayne Rainey
d. Barry Sheene

4. Recognized as "Steady Eddie" for his consistent and swift performance, this rider secured all four of his 500cc Grand Prix championship titles during the 1980s. What is his surname?
   a. Russell
   b. Lawson
   c. Schwantz
   d. Mamola

5. Renowned for his aggressive riding approach, Japanese World Superbike rider Noriyuki Haga displays the number 41 on his motorcycle. By what nickname or nicknames is he known?
   a. Nitro Nori
   b. Samurai of Slide
   c. Both are wrong
   d. Both are correct

6. Accumulating three AMA Superbike championship titles and two World Superbike championship titles, the rider known as "Flyin' Fred" is identified by what last name?
   a. Fogarty
   b. Merkel
   c. Slight
   d. Chandler

7. What nickname is associated with the multiple world champion Freddie Spencer?
   a. Speedy Spencer
   b. Fleet Freddie
   c. Fred the First

d. Fast Freddie

8. What nickname is commonly attributed to the legendary multiple world champion, Mike Hailwood?
a. The Bike
b. Sir Speed
c. The Quick
d. The King

9. What is the nickname or nicknames of Nicky Hayden, the 2006 MotoGP world champion?
a. Kentucky Kid
b. Trick Daddy
c. Both are wrong
d. Both are correct

10. Hailing from Rome, Italy, this four-time 250cc Grand Prix world champion is recognized by the nicknames "Roman Emperor" and "Mad Max." Who is he?
a. Pierfrancesco Chili
b. Loris Capirossi
c. Max Biaggi
d. Marco Melandri

Answers

1. Valentino Rossi
2. Colin Edwards
3. Kenny Roberts Sr.
4. Lawson

5. Both are correct
6. Merkel
7. Fast Freddie
8. The Bike
9. Both are correct
10. Max Biaggi

Speedway. Identifying League Team Nicknames

1. What is the nickname of the inaugural official team, established in 1928, that operated at both Hyde Road and Kirkmanshulme Lane?
a. Aces
b. Eagles
c. Pirates
d. Bulldogs

2. Established in 1948 and notably acquiring Jason Crump for the 2007 season, this team, affiliated with over 340 different points-scoring riders, claims to have defeated Coventry 56 times, as per their website. What is the nickname of this team?
a. Eagles
b. Bulldogs
c. Witches
d. Pirates

3. Situated at the East of England showground, this Elite League team features one of the largest tracks in the UK. Originating in 1970, they continue to operate to this day.
   a. Panthers
   b. Eagles
   c. Pirates
   d. Diamonds

4. Founded in 1931 and located in Arlington, Sussex, which team, boasting blue and yellow colors, stands as one of the oldest teams in operation?
   a. Cheetahs
   b. Silver Machine
   c. Eagles
   d. Bulldogs

5. Emerging in 1984 to fill a twelve-year speedway void in their county, this team adopted their nickname from one of the three teams replaced by them. Subsequently, they have undergone a change in track name. What is the nickname of this team?
   a. Clubs
   b. Rockets
   c. Cheetahs
   d. Hammers

6. Originally situated at a location now transformed into a football ground, this team relocated in the 1950s. When their original track was paved over for a stock car circuit, they responded by constructing a new

track indoors. What is the nickname of this enduring team?
a. Tigers
b. Witches
c. Silver Machine
d. Cheetahs

7. Similar to The Belle Vue Aces, this team was established in 1928 in Brandon and has consistently raced there, in contrast to their early counterparts, the Aces, who had to relocate. What is the nickname of this team?
a. Bullets
b. Wasps
c. Bulldogs
d. Bees

8. Commencing in April 1939, this team participated in racing in 1940 and part of 1941 before being suspended during the war. Racing recommenced in 1949 following track alterations. At times, they have fielded two teams, one in the Elite League and the other in the Conference League. A single nickname has remained associated with them throughout. What is that nickname?
a. Silver Machine
b. Cheetahs
c. Rhinos
d. Lions

9. Ascending to the Elite League in 2006, this team relinquished their 'Racers' nickname in favor of a new

one. Established in 1968, they played their inaugural match at a greyhound stadium, securing victory against the Nelson Admirals. What is the nickname of this team?

a. Robins
b. Bulldogs
c. Tigers
d. Lions

10. Boasting over 59 years of competition in the top speedway leagues, this team has achieved a unique feat by consistently racing at the same track, a distinction unmatched by any other team. Commencing their first race in 1949, what is the nickname of this enduring team?

a. Robins
b. Sparrows
c. Eagles
d. Hawks

Answers

1. Aces
2. Pirates
3. Panthers
4. Eagles
5. Hammers
6. Witches
7. Bees
8. Cheetahs
9. Bulldogs

10.   Robins

TT Races on the Isle of Man

1. When was the transition from the St. John's course to the mountain course for the Isle of Man TT Races, which initially took place in 1907?
   a. 1915
   b. 1911
   c. 1919
   d. 1924

2. Which rider achieved the milestone of the first 100mph lap in 1957 as speeds continued to rise each year?
   a. Mike Hailwood
   b. Geoff Duke
   c. Bob McIntyre
   d. Phil Read

3. In 1985, Joey Dunlop, a legendary TT rider, faced a potential obstacle that nearly prevented him from participating in the races. What was the reason for this challenge?
   a. He was shipwrecked
   b. He forgot to register in time
   c. He was in a car accident
   d. He was struck down with food poisoning

4. What is the name of the mountain over which the course reaches its highest point?
   a. Snaplie
   b. Snowdon
   c. Snaefell
   d. Shapfelt

5. What is the total length of the contemporary TT course?
   a. 30-1/2 miles
   b. 37-3/4 miles
   c. 27-1/4 miles
   d. 40-3/4 miles

6. Among the various jumps on the course, one stands out as particularly famous, located over a small bridge in a village. What is the name of this renowned jump?
   a. Creg Ny Ba
   b. Governor
   c. Ballaugh
   d. Ballacraine

7. Given that the race takes place on public roads, riders face numerous obstacles on the course. What specific obstacle do they encounter at the bungalow?
   a. Cattle grid
   b. Hairpin bend
   c. Tram tracks
   d. Stone walls

8. Which manufacturer established a dedicated racing team with the sole purpose of winning the Isle of Man TT races?
a. Ducati
b. Honda
c. Yamaha
d. Gilera

9. What is the traditional practice that many riders commonly follow, believing it brings them luck?
a. Say hello to the fairies at the fairy bridge
b. Try to stroke a Manx cat
c. Carry a fourleaf clover on the bike
d. Wear the same underwear for the whole period

10. What led to the cancellation of the entire event in 2001?
a. Snow on the mountain section
b. Foot and mouth disease outbreak in the UK
c. Road subsidence at Kirkmichael
d. Ferry workers strike

Answers

1. 1911
2. Bob McIntyre
3. He was shipwrecked
4. Snaefell
5. 37-3/4 miles
6. Ballaugh

7. Tram tracks
8. Honda
9. Say hello to the fairies at the fairy bridge
10. Foot and mouth disease outbreak in the UK

Isle Be Back

1. Which team did the Italian rider Tarquinio Provini secure the majority of his four Isle of Man TT wins with?
a. MV Agusta
b. Benilli
c. Mondial
d. Kreidler

2. Of the years mentioned, which one is not among the hat-trick years for the Northern Irish rider Joey Dunlop, who achieved a total of 26 wins in various classes at the Isle of Man TT races?
a. 1985
b. 2000
c. 1988
d. 1983

3. Carl Fogarty, a four-time World Superbike title holder, secured three wins at the Isle of Man TT. How many years did his lap record endure before Jim Moodie broke it in 1999?
a. 4
b. 8

c. 7
d. 5

4. In 1930 to 1937, Jimmy Guthrie clinched six Isle of Man TT victories, with five of them aboard Norton motorcycles. In which country did he tragically lose his life while racing in 1937?
   a. Holland
   b. Germany
   c. Spain
   d. Norway

5. Mike Hailwood, famously known as "Mike the Bike," achieved fourteen Isle of Man TT titles and made a rare transition from two to four wheels. What is the name of the trophy he received, a prestigious honor also held by Richard Branson, Amy Johnson, and Donald Campbell?
   a. Segrave Trophy
   b. Eglinton Trophy
   c. Claret Jug
   d. America's Cup

6. During his three Isle of Man TT victories, what was the name of the team that William Raymond Amm, born in Salisbury, Southern Rhodesia, rode for?
   a. Honda
   b. MV Agusta
   c. Norton
   d. Vespa

7. During the Isle of Man TT races, Stanley Woods, a ten-time winner, used to treat the Boy Scouts. What was the specific treat he would give them?
   a. Chocolate
   b. Toffee
   c. Cookies
   d. Sherbet

8. In 2010, Ian Hutchinson secured victories in five Isle of Man TT races, excluding the sidecar events. Which specific race did he not participate in during that year?
   a. TT Zero
   b. Superstock TT
   c. Superbike TT
   d. Senior TT

9. Before John Surtees transitioned to Formula 1 in 1960, how many Isle of Man TT races did he win as the first person to achieve World Championships on both two and four wheels?
   a. 6
   b. 9
   c. 2
   d. 14

10. In which year did Dave Molyneux, a native of the Isle of Man, secure his first victory in the Isle of Man TT races for sidecars?
   a. 1985
   b. 1988
   c. 1987

d. 1989

Answers

1. MV Agusta
2. 1983
3. 7
4. Germany
5. Segrave Trophy
6. Norton
7. Toffee
8. TT Zero
9. 6
10. 1989

Valentino Rossi. Forza Dottore Trivia

1. What is the Birthplace and Birthdate of Valentino Rossi?
   a. 5 May 1980, Perugia
   b. 13 January 1977, Rome
   c. 16 February 1979, Urbino
   d. 23 July 1975, Urbino

2. In which country did he start his career in the Championship?

a. Italy
b. Spain
c. France
d. Germany

3. True or False: His father, who also rode motorcycles competitively, was very happy that Valentino wanted to follow his steps in motorcycling when he was a child.
a. True
b. False

4. With which one of these riders does he have a very "tense" relationship?
a. Carlos Checa
b. Noriyuki Abe
c. Loris Capirossi
d. Max Biaggi

5. In which year did Valentino Rossi win the 250 cc Championship?
a. 1997
b. 1998
c. 1999
d. 2000

6. True or False: Mick Doohan became Vale's team adviser in 2000.
a. True
b. False

7. What did Valentino Rossi have for a "racemate" when he raced MiniMotorbikes?
a. A Photo of his Dog
b. A Doll

c. A Ninja Turtle
d. A Cap with a Comb

8. When did Valentino Rossi win his first MotoGP Championship?
a. 28 August 2001
b. 21 September 2002
c. 15 June 2000
d. 23 September 2002

9. Which of these is one of his tattoos?
a. A Girl
b. A Car
c. A Motorcycle
d. A Turtle

10. When Valentino Rossi first raced in the World Championship, what number did he use?
a. 7
b. 3
c. 46
d. 65

11. What firm was Valentino Rossi riding for when he won his two first world championships?
a. Honda
b. Aprillia
c. Yamaha
d. Gilera

12. Which was the last race did Valentino Rossi has won in 02-03 season?
a. Australia
b. Japan-Motegi
c. Malaysia
d. Brazil

13. True or False: Valentino Rossi favorite circuit is Japan-Suzuka.
   a. True
   b. False

14. What is the name of Valentino Rossi's dog, whose picture he displayed in front of the number 1 when securing the 2003 MOTOGP Championship?
   a. Guido
   b. Gianni
   c. Mario
   d. Max

15. True or False: Valentino Rossi doesn't accept to have tobacco advertisements on his moto or on his overall.
   a. True
   b. False

Answers

1. 16 February 1979, Urbino
2. Spain
3. False
4. Max Biaggi
5. 1999
6. True
7. A Ninja Turtle
8. 21 September 2002
9. A Turtle
10. 46
11. Aprillia
12. Australia
13. false

14. Guido
15. False

A Long Time Ago. Giacomo Agostini Trivia!

1. In which city was Giacomo Agostini born? It's the same city where the Mille Miglia classic and vintage cars race starts from.
   a. Palermo
   b. Modena
   c. Brescia
   d. Milano

2. Giacomo Agostini started in 190 Grand Prix races. How many of them did he win?
   a. 99
   b. 118
   c. 123
   d. 100

3. Young Ago (Giacomo Agostini) required his father's signature to participate in races. How did he manage to obtain it?
   a. His father had a dream in which he saw Ago becoming World Champion.
   b. The father was an ardent fan of motorcycle races
   c. The father believed it was signing for a bicycle race.
   d. He falsified it

4. What motorcycle did Ago use to secure victory in the Italian Juniores Speed 175 cc Championship in 1963?
   a. Ducati
   b. Benelli

c. Morini
   d. BMW

5. In 1965, Ago began competing in the World Grand Prix Championship, participating in the 350cc and 500cc classes. For a continuous span of nine years, he rode an Italian motorcycle in both categories. Which specific Italian motorcycle did he ride?
   a. Moto Guzzi
   b. Ducati
   c. MV Agusta
   d. Benelli

6. In 1974, Ago emerged victorious in which renowned American racing event?
   a. Riverside
   b. Loudon Classic
   c. Daytona 200
   d. Laguna Seca

7. In 1970, Ago secured victory in 19 races, a record he shares with which other legendary British motorcyclist?
   a. Mike Hailwood
   b. Phil Read
   c. John Surtees
   d. Geoff Duke

8. How did Ago fare at the Isle of Man Tourist Trophy in 1973?
   a. He won
   b. He refused to race.
   c. He retired for a mechanical problem
   d. He fell and injured himself

9. Ago had a notable adversary, an Italian racer who met a tragic end in Monza in 1973. He shared the same surname as a renowned Italian film director, **Renzo** _____.
   a. Fellini
   b. Leone
   c. Antonioni
   d. Pasolini

10. Ago concluded his motorcycle racing career in 1977, having clinched 15 Grand Prix Championships. Subsequently, he explored various professions. In which of these pursuits did he NOT test his luck?
    a. Car racing
    b. Singer
    c. Actor
    d. Team Manager

Answers

1. Brescia
2. 123
3. The father believed it was signing for a bicycle race.
4. Morini
5. MV Agusta
6. Daytona 200
7. Mike Hailwood
8. He refused to race.
9. Pasolini
10. Singer

Travis Pastrana Trivia

1. What is Travis's date of birth?
a. October 10, 1982
b. October 8, 1982
c. October 9, 1983
d. October 8, 1983

2. In which location was Travis born?
a. Annapolis, MD
b. Baton Rouge, LA
c. Anadarko, OK
d. Daytona, FL

3. At what age did Travis begin riding his first bike, a single-speed Honda Z-50?
a. seven
b. ten
c. four
d. six

4. How many instances did he secure the title of Loretta Lynn National Amateur Champion?
a. Three times
b. Five times
c. Eight times
d. Once

5. Which of the following riders was Travis Pastrana's partner when he won the doubles gold medal at the 1999 Gravity Games?
a. Brian Deegan
b. Carey Hart

c. Mike Metzger
d. Kenny Bartram

6. At what age did Travis Pastrana secure his first freestyle championship victory?
a. 14
b. 10
c. 17
d. 15

7. According to TravisPastrana.com, what nickname do his friends use for him when he's armed with a paintball gun?
a. Just plain Travis
b. Killer
c. Travenator
d. None of these

8. How many years ahead of schedule did Travis finish high school?
a. One
b. He didn't finish early
c. Four
d. Two

9. True or False: Travis has multiple tattoos, including an image of his bike on one arm, and six piercings in each ear.
a. True
b. False

10. What event did he earn gold in at the 2001 Gravity Games?
a. 125 Freestyle
b. 250 Supercross
c. 125 Supercross
d. 250 Freestyle

Answers

1. October 8, 1983
2. Annapolis, MD
3. four
4. Five times
5. Kenny Bartram
6. 14
7. Travenator
8. Two
9. False
10. 250 Freestyle

Speedway - From The Beginning!

1. Speedway has been a longstanding and popular motorsport in Britain, with its origins dating back many years. Can you identify the year when the first-ever speedway meeting took place in Britain?
   a. 1889
   b. 1913
   c. 1901
   d. 1928

2. The bikes used in today's speedway racing have undergone minimal changes since the sport's inception. They significantly deviate from regular motorbikes in

two crucial aspects. What are the two components absent from a speedway bike?
a. Tyre Tread and Mud Guards
b. Silencer and Mirrors
c. Clutch and Speedometer
d. Brakes and Gears

3. All speedway bikes must adhere to the regulations set by the governing body, the FIM. What is the mandated engine size for all speedway bikes?
a. 250cc
b. 800cc
c. 600cc
d. 500cc

4. During the early days of speedway, a handful of pioneering riders played a crucial role in popularizing the sport by touring various regions and entertaining growing crowds. Among these names, which individual was not among the original speedway riders?
a. Racer Harris
b. Skid Plevin
c. Buster Breaks
d. Slider Shuttleworth

5. As speedway gained popularity, a league was established in 1929. Among these Midlands cities, which one did not have a team in this inaugural league?
a. Leicester
b. Coventry
c. Birmingham
d. Wolverhampton

6. During the inaugural speedway season in 1929, there were northern and southern leagues. While Leeds claimed the northern league title, which team emerged victorious in the southern league?
   a. White Hart Lane
   b. Stamford Bridge
   c. Highbury
   d. Wembley

7. What was the attendance for the 1938 World Final Championships held at Wembley, which set the record for the largest crowd at a speedway meeting in Britain?
   a. 26,000
   b. 62,000
   c. 44,000
   d. 93,000

8. Among the notable speedway riders throughout the years, can you identify the club that Cyril Maidment, Ove Fundin, Soren Sjosten, and Ivan Mauger all rode for?
   a. Halifax
   b. Swindon
   c. Eastbourne
   d. Belle Vue

9. Speedway in Scotland experienced early success with numerous races held, including the first one at Celtic Park. Among the options provided, which team was not a genuine Scottish side during that period?
   a. Paisley Lions
   b. Edinburgh Monarchs
   c. Glasgow Tigers

d. Coatbridge Coyotes

10. Among the listed riders, which pair is not genuinely composed of brothers in speedway history?
a. Ales and Lukas Dryml
b. Ray and Vic Duggan
c. Peter and Phil Collins
d. Charlie and Alf Parker

Answers

1. 1928
2. Brakes and Gears
3. 500cc
4. Racer Harris
5. Wolverhampton
6. Stamford Bridge
7. 93,000
8. Belle Vue
9. Coatbridge Coyotes
10. Charlie and Alf Parker

Speedway Team's Nicknames

1. By what nickname is Belle Vue commonly known?
a. Lightning
b. Storm
c. Aces
d. Wolves

2. What is the commonly used nickname for the Polish team Gniezno?
   a. TZ Stop
   b. TZ Start
   c. TZ Turnaround
   d. TZ Backward

3. Which team was referred to by the nicknames Knights, Silver Machine, and Stars?
   a. Oxford
   b. Buxton
   c. Newport
   d. Kings Lynn

4. Which nickname is common to Glasgow, Mildenhall, Sheffield, and the now-defunct Cornish side Trelawny?
   a. Tigers
   b. Falcons
   c. Lions
   d. Rangers

5. The Polonia Stadium serves as the regular venue for the Polish Grand Prix and is also the home ground for a team nicknamed Polonia. What is the name of this team?
   a. Bydgoszcz
   b. Gdansk
   c. Wroclaw
   d. Warsaw

6. Which British league team has the same nickname as the Swedish league outfit Motala?
   a. Poole

b. Rye House
c. Eastbourne
d. Isle Of Wight

7. What is the commonly used nickname for the Polish team Torun?
a. Raptor
b. Polonia
c. Wisla
d. Sport

8. What is the commonly used nickname for Buxton's Speedway Team?
a. Bandits
b. Outlaws
c. Robbers
d. Hitmen

9. Which two British clubs are known by nicknames that are flying insects?
a. Armadale and Stoke
b. Coventry and Newport
c. Reading and Swindon
d. Peterborough and Somerset

10. Which British team is the sole one to feature a marine animal in its name?
a. Ipswich
b. Newcastle
c. Carmarthen
d. Boston

Answers

1. Aces
2. TZ Start
3. Kings Lynn
4. Tigers
5. Bydgoszcz
6. Poole
7. Raptor
8. Hitmen
9. Coventry and Newport
10. Boston

Supercross Trivia

1. Among the given riders, who achieved the feat of winning a supercross race in both the 250 class and the 125 class in the same season?
   a. Jeremy McGrath
   b. Kevin Whindam
   c. Ricky Carmichael
   d. Ezra Lusk

2. Who, aside from Jeremy McGrath, was the sole rider to secure a victory in a 250 Supercross event during the 1996 season?
   a. Greg Albertyn

b. Ezra Lusk
c. Jeff Emig
d. Bob Hannah

3. Which individual, previously victorious in 125 Supercross races, has now become a prominent figure in the Moto-X freestyle realm and leads 'the metal mulisha'?
   a. Casey Johnson
   b. Nathan Ramsey
   c. Brian Deegan
   d. Travis Pastrana

4. Which two riders clinched the 125 East and West titles for the 2000 season?
   a. Shae Bentley and Travis Pastrana
   b. Shae Bentley and Stephane Roncada
   c. Stephane Roncada and Nathan Ramsey
   d. Travis Pastrana and Ricky Carmichael

5. How many races did Ezra Lusk emerge victorious in during the 2000 Supercross season?
   a. one
   b. two
   c. none
   d. Four

6. Up until December 2000, how many 250 Supercross Championships had Jeremy McGrath secured?
   a. seven
   b. eight
   c. six
   d. Four

7. Has Larry Ward ever won a 250 Supercross race?

a. Yes
b. No

8. Who served as Jeremy McGrath's main competitor for the 2000 Supercross season championship?
a. Jeff Emig
b. David Vuillemin
c. Ricky Carmichael
d. Kevin Whindam

9. Which former Supercross champion has transitioned to racing cars in the IRL series?
a. Jeff Ward
b. Rick Johnson
c. Larry Ward
d. Damon Bradshaw

10. Which former Supercross champion shifted his skills to GP Motorcycle Road racing?
a. Jean-Michel Bayle
b. Donnie Schmit
c. Kevin Schwantz
d. Jeff Ward

Answers

1. Kevin Whindam
2. Jeff Emig
3. Brian Deegan
4. Shae Bentley and Stephane Roncada
5. none
6. seven
7. Yes

8. David Vuillemin
9. Jeff Ward
10. Jean-Michel Bayle

ATV Trivia

1. Which company manufactured the V-Force 700?
   a. Polaris
   b. Kawasaki
   c. Suzuki
   d. Bombardier

2. Which manufacturer produced the Outlander 400/330?
   a. Polaris
   b. Bombardier
   c. Arctic Cat
   d. Honda

3. Did Honda produce the 250, 300, and 400 EX models?
   a. Yes
   b. No

4. True or False: Polaris manufacture the Raptor 350/660
   a. True
   b. False

5. Which company produced the DVX 400?
   a. Polaris

b. Arctic Cat
c. Suzuki
d. KMT

6. Which company manufactured the Predator 500/90/50?
a. Kawasaki
b. Honda
c. Polaris
d. Yamaha

7. Which company produced the Rally 200?
a. Bombardier
b. Honda
c. Suzuki
d. Yamaha

8. Who made the Twin Peaks 700?
a. Yamaha
b. Kawasaki
c. Suzuki
d. Honda

9. Which company manufactured the Phoenix 200?
a. Honda
b. Polaris
c. KMT
d. Kawasaki

10. Which company is credited with inventing the ATV (All-Terrain Vehicle)?
a. Honda
b. Polaris
c. Suzuki
d. Bombardier

Answers

1. Kawasaki
2. Bombardier
3. Yes
4. False
5. Arctic Cat
6. Polaris
7. Bombardier
8. Suzuki
9. Polaris
10. Suzuki

Motorcycle Road Racing Trivia

1. In the year 2000, which brand of motorcycle did Scott Russell ride?
   a. Kawasaki
   b. Harley Davidson
   c. Ducati
   d. Yamaha

2. True or false: Colin Edwards raced in the AMA 250GP class early in his career?
   a. True
   b. False

3. Which motorcycle brand did John Kocinski ride to victory in a World Superbike Championship?
   a. Suzuki
   b. Ducati
   c. Honda
   d. Yamaha

4. True or False: Doug Chandler, Jamie James, Ben Bostrom, and Anthony Gobert have all won the AMA Superbike Championship points title?
   a. True
   b. False

5. Which racetrack is famously referred to as 'The fastest Road in the West'?
   a. Willow Springs
   b. Sears Point
   c. Phoenix International Raceway
   d. California Speedway

6. Among the following riders, who has a higher number of AMA Superbike race victories?
   a. Nicky Hayden
   b. Colin Edwards
   c. Miguel Duhamel
   d. Ben Bostrom

7. Which individual is commonly known by the nickname 'Mr. Daytona'?
   a. Scott Russell
   b. Miquel Duhamel
   c. Dale Earnhardt
   d. Eddie Lawson

8. Which rider, tragically, won his initial AMA 600 Supersport Final at Mid-Ohio Sports Car Course but met with a fatal crash during the Superbike race on the same day?
   a. Jimmy Adamo
   b. Davey Allison
   c. Jamie Bowman
   d. Larry Schwarzbach

9. What term or nickname, shared by Eddie Lawson and certain other two-stroke Grand Prix riders, is used to refer to a four-stroke race bike and its engine?
   a. thunder
   b. nightmare
   c. rattler
   d. Diesel

10. Which 500 Grand Prix rider secured victory in the first 500 Grand Prix race he entered?
   a. Kenny Roberts
   b. Kevin Schwantz
   c. Max Biaggi
   d. Valentino Rossi

Answers

1. Harley Davidson
2. True
3. Honda
4. false
5. Willow Springs
6. Miguel Duhamel

7. Scott Russell
8. Larry Schwarzbach
9. diesel
10. Max Biaggi

Swindon Speedway 2008

1. Against which team did Swindon face defeat in the playoffs?
   a. Lakeside Hammers
   b. Coventry Bees
   c. Poole Pirates
   d. Ipswich Witches

2. Which rider achieved a remarkable 21-point maximum during the Robins' 49-41 victory over Lakeside at Arena Essex?
   a. Jurica Pavlic
   b. Troy Batchelor
   c. Leigh Adams
   d. Mads Korneliussen

3. Which rider among these did not achieve a maximum score in the year 2008?
   a. Leigh Adams
   b. Troy Batchelor
   c. Mads Korneliussen
   d. Jurica Pavlic

4. In which Australian city was Swindon rider Troy Batchelor born?

a. Sydney
b. Perth
c. Melbourne
d. Brisbane

5. **Who did Jurica Pavlic substitute for as a replacement for an injured Swindon Robins rider in 2008?**
a. Theo Pijper
b. Troy Batchelor
c. Sebastian Alden
d. Travis McGowan

6. **In 2008, which competition did Swindon emerge victorious in?**
a. Elite Shield
b. Craven Shield
c. Elite League Pairs
d. Knock Out Cup

7. **Which team managed to defeat Swindon twice in the Elite League at the Abbey Stadium in 2008?**
a. Belle Vue Aces
b. Lakeside Hammers
c. Poole Pirates
d. Ipswich Witches

8. **During 2008, how many victories did Swindon secure in away matches?**
a. 5
b. 3
c. 4
d. 6

9. **What was the total number of points that Swindon accumulated at the conclusion of the season?**

a. 40
b. 41
c. 37
d. 44

10. On his debut for the Robins, Manuel Hauzinger defeated which Grand Prix rider?
a. Bjarne Pedersen
b. Freddie Lindgren
c. Scott Nicholls
d. Niels-Kristian Iversen

Answers

1. Lakeside Hammers
2. Jurica Pavlic
3. Mads Korneliussen
4. Brisbane
5. Sebastian Alden
6. Elite Shield
7. 5
8. 41
9. Scott Nicholls

British Speedway 2009

1. In 2009, which team emerged as the league champions?
a. Ipswich Witches

b. Wolverhampton Wolves
   c. Swindon Robins
   d. Lakeside Hammers

2. **Which rider among these concluded the season with the highest average at its conclusion?**
   a. Leigh Adams
   b. Matej Zagar
   c. Hans Andersen
   d. Freddie Lindgren

3. **Who experienced the most significant improvement in their average during the 2009 season?**
   a. Tai Woffinden
   b. Ben Barker
   c. Kenneth Hansen
   d. Patrick Hougaard

4. **Who witnessed the most substantial decrease in their average during the 2009 season?**
   a. Bjarne Pedersen
   b. Davey Watt
   c. Charlie Gjedde
   d. Adam Shields

5. **Which team concluded the league without facing a defeat in home matches?**
   a. Peterborough Panthers
   b. Swindon Robins
   c. Wolverhampton Wolves
   d. Lakeside Hammers

6. **Who emerged as the champion of the Elite League Riders Championship?**
   a. Chris Harris

b. Freddie Lindgren
   c. Leigh Adams
   d. Chris Holder

7. Which team, in their 2009 lineup, was the sole one that did not include a British rider?
   a. Peterborough Panthers
   b. Poole Pirates
   c. Swindon Robins
   d. Lakeside Hammers

8. According to the final greensheet averages in 2009, who held the position of the top British rider?
   a. Chris Harris
   b. Scott Nicholls
   c. Tai Woffinden
   d. Lee Richardson

9. Who secured victory in the British Final that took place at Poole's Wimborne Road Stadium?
   a. Scott Nicholls
   b. Chris Harris
   c. Edward Kennett
   d. Lee Richardson

10. Excluding guests, how many riders represented the Swindon Robins in 2009?
    a. 11
    b. 14
    c. 12
    d. 13

Answers

1. Swindon Robins

2. Freddie Lindgren
3. Ben Barker
4. Charlie Gjedde
5. Wolverhampton Wolves
6. Leigh Adams
7. Peterborough Panthers
8. Lee Richardson
9. Chris Harris
10. 13

Road Bike Racing in 2003

1. Which British rider lost his life in a helicopter accident in 2003?
   a. Barry Sheene
   b. Steve Hislop
   c. David Jefferies
   d. Carl Fogarty

2. Who emerged as the victor in both World Superbike races at Brands Hatch in 2003?
   a. Neil Hodgson
   b. Shane Byrne
   c. Ruben Xaus
   d. Chris Walker

3. True or False: James Toseland scored his first World Superbike race win at Silverstone?
   a. True
   b. False

4. What was the significance of Neil Hodgson's number 100?
   a. It stood for he was number 1 in the year 2000
   b. He was celebrating his 100th race this year
   c. He was celebrating his 100th win this year
   d. He thought that it would make him stand out

5. What was the total number of points Valentino Rossi earned in the MotoGP championship in 2003?
   a. 357
   b. 356
   c. 350
   d. 360

6. What was the total points tally for Neil Hodgson in the World Superbike Championship in 2003?
   a. 489
   b. 480
   c. 488
   d. 490

7. From the beginning of the 2003 championship, how many consecutive wins did Neil Hodgson secure?
   a. 9
   b. 8
   c. 10
   d. 7

8. How many races did Valentino Rossi triumph in throughout the entirety of the 2003 season?
   a. 11
   b. 7
   c. 9
   d. 10

9. Who clinched the world 250cc championship?
a. Sebastian Porto
b. Roberto Rolfo
c. Toni Elias
d. Manuel Poggiali

10. Who emerged as the victor in the 125cc World Championship?
a. Daniel Pedrosa
b. Alex De Angelis
c. Hector Barbera
d. Pablo Nieto

Answers

1. Steve Hislop
2. Shane Byrne
3. False
4. It stood for he was number 1 in the year 2000
5. 357
6. 489
7. 9
8. 9
9. Manuel Poggiali
10. Daniel Pedrosa

Freestyle Motocross

1. How many members did the Metal Mulisha have in the 20th century?

a. 3
b. 2
c. 1
d. 6

2. Which individual leaped over his parents' house for an MTV commercial?
a. Carey Hart
b. Mike Metzger
c. Trevor Vines
d. Mike Cinqmars

3. Which rider attempted to surpass the world jump record in 1999 but ended up crashing?
a. Mike Cinqmars
b. Seth Enslow
c. Mike Metzger
d. Carey Hart

4. Which individual successfully executed the first-ever backflip on a 250 motocross bike?
a. Mike Metzger
b. Carey Hart
c. Travis Pastrana
d. Mike Cinqmars

5. After executing the first-ever backflip on a 250 motocross bike, what position did the rider achieve in the competition?
a. 10th
b. 3rd
c. 1st
d. 13th

6. Who formed the other half of the Metzger Motorsports freestyle team?
   a. Carey Hart
   b. Travis Pastrana
   c. Seth Enslow
   d. Reagan Seig

7. For which team did Cliff Adoptante ride in the late 1990s?
   a. Fox Racing
   b. LBZ
   c. Oakley
   d. Thor

8. Which of these individuals was NOT a member of MotoXXX?
   a. Tommy Clowers
   b. Mike Cinqmars
   c. Trevor Vines
   d. Kyle Lewis

9. True or False: Travis Pastrana won the 1999 Gravity Games, the 1999 X-Games, and the 2000 Gravity Games.
   a. True
   b. False

10. True or False: Travis broke his brake lever trying to pull a backflip at the 2000 X-games.
    a. True
    b. False

11. In the freestyle video "Throttle Junkies," what number adorned Mike Metzger's bike?
    a. 52

b. 1
  c. 46
  d. 65

12. In the freestyle video "Throttle Junkies," which brand of bike did Mike Metzger ride?
  a. Suzuki
  b. Kawasaki
  c. Yamaha
  d. Honda

13. True or False: Mike Metzger used to ride for Orange County Suzuki.
  a. True
  b. False

14. True or False: Brian Deegan used to race a Chapparal backed Yamaha?
  a. True
  b. False

15. Which individual made an appearance in a Kid Rock video?
  a. Travis Pastrana
  b. Carey Hart
  c. Seth Enslow
  d. Mike Cinqmars

16. True or False: Mike Metzger invented a trick called 'The Mcrib'.
  a. True
  b. False

17. True or False: Kenny Bartram invented the 'Cordova'.

a. True
b. False

18. What is the middle name of Mike Metzger?
a. Tom
b. James
c. Cletus
d. Fritz

19. What type of motorcycle did Cliff Adoptante ride?
a. Kawasaki
b. Honda
c. Husqvarna
d. Suzuki

20. The 'Rodeo Heel Clicker' involves tossing both legs to one side of the bike while exclaiming "Yee Haw!!!"
a. True
b. False

Answers

1. 2
2. Mike Cinqmars
3. Seth Enslow
4. Carey Hart
5. 10th
6. Reagan Seig
7. LBZ
8. Trevor Vines
9. False

10. False
11. 65
12. Kawasaki
13. True
14. False
15. Seth Enslow
16. False
17. False
18. Fritz
19. Suzuki
20. False

The Berwick Bandits

1. When were the Bandits initially established?
a. 1968
b. 1961
c. 1969
d. 1975

2. Berwick Bandits have had two permanent homes in their speedway history; Shielfield Park is one, but what is the other?
a. Berrington Lough
b. Brough Park
c. Powder Hall
d. Derwent Park

3. Who earned the title of 'Bandit of the Season' for the year 2003?
a. Carlos Villar

b. Paul Bentley
c. Michal Makovsky
d. David Meldrum

4. On which night of the week do Berwick typically hold their races?
a. Friday
b. Saturday
c. Sunday
d. Monday

5. Did Berwick secure the League championship in 1992?
a. True
b. False

Answers

1. 1968
2. Berrington Lough
3. David Meldrum
4. Saturday
5. False

Motorcycle In Cinema

1. In the movie "Easy Rider" (1969), what iconic motorcycle do the main characters ride?
a. Harley-Davidson Sportster
b. Honda CB750
c. Triumph Bonneville

d. Ducati Monster

2. **Which film features a futuristic motorcycle called the Light Cycle?**
   a. Tron
   b. Blade Runner
   c. Mad Max: Fury Road
   d. The Matrix

3. **In "The Great Escape" (1963), what motorcycle jump scene became legendary?**
   a. BMW R75
   b. Harley-Davidson Knucklehead
   c. Triumph TR6 Trophy
   d. Indian Scout

4. **Who played the iconic role of the Ghost Rider in the movie "Ghost Rider" (2007)?**
   a. Keanu Reeves
   b. Nicolas Cage
   c. Wesley Snipes
   d. Hugh Jackman

5. **Which motorcycle brand is prominently featured in the film "The Wild One" (1953)?**
   a. Yamaha
   b. Harley-Davidson
   c. Ducati
   d. Kawasaki

6. **Which movie features a gang of bikers known as the War Boys, riding heavily modified motorcycles in a post-apocalyptic world?**
   a. Mad Max: Fury Road
   b. The Road Warrior
   c. Death Race 2000

d. Escape from New York

7. In the film "Terminator 2: Judgment Day" (1991), what type of motorcycle does the Terminator ride during the iconic chase scene?
   a. Honda CBR600
   b. Kawasaki Ninja
   c. Harley-Davidson Fat Boy
   d. Yamaha YZF-R1

8. What motorcycle does Tom Cruise ride in the movie "Top Gun" (1986)?
   a. Kawasaki Ninja ZX-6R
   b. Suzuki GSX-R750
   c. Honda CB750
   d. Kawasaki GPZ900R

9. Which film features a motorcycle-riding vigilante anti-hero who dispenses his own form of justice in the fictional Mega-City One?
   a. Judge Dredd
   b. The Punisher
   c. Sin City
   d. V for Vendetta

10. In "The Dark Knight" (2008), what motorcycle does Batman use to chase down the Joker?
    a. Batpod
    b. Batcycle
    c. Nightstalker
    d. Shadowfax

11. Which actor portrayed the character Johnny Blaze in the film "Ghost Rider: Spirit of Vengeance" (2011)?
    a. Matt Damon

b. Ryan Reynolds
c. Nicolas Cage
d. Jared Leto

12. What motorcycle brand is associated with the character Marlon Brando played in "The Wild One" (1953)?
a. Triumph
b. Indian
c. Norton
d. BSA

13. Which film features a motorcycle-riding hitman seeking revenge for his dog's death?
a. John Wick
b. Taken
c. The Equalizer
d. Kill Bill

14. In the movie "The Motorcycle Diaries" (2004), what type of motorcycle do the main characters ride across South America?
a. Harley-Davidson Sportster
b. BMW R1200GS
c. Honda CB500
d. Norton Commando

15. Which film features a time-traveling cyborg sent to protect a young John Connor, who learns to ride a motorcycle in the process?
a. Terminator 3: Rise of the Machines
b. Terminator Salvation
c. Terminator Genisys
d. Terminator Dark Fate

Answers

1. Triumph Bonneville
2. Tron
3. Triumph TR6 Trophy
4. Nicolas Cage
5. Harley-Davidson
6. Mad Max: Fury Road
7. Harley-Davidson Fat Boy
8. Kawasaki GPZ900R
9. Judge Dredd
10. Batpod
11. Nicolas Cage
12. Triumph
13. John Wick
14. BMW R1200GS
15. Terminator 3: Rise of the Machines

Manufactured by Amazon.ca
Bolton, ON